www.BraveSmartandBeautiful.com

Dear Margarita,
You inspire me.
I have learned so much from you. I'm so blessed to call you friend! Now its time I make you proud! Thank you for everything
Love Ya!
Diane

Copyright©2016 by Diane Grant. All rights reserved. No part of this publication may be reproduced, distributed, or transmitted in any form or by any means, including photocopying, recording, or other electronic or mechanical methods, without the prior written permission of the author except in the case of brief quotations embodied in critical reviews and certain other noncommercial uses permitted by copyright law.
For permission requests,
write to: **Diane@BraveSmartandBeautiful.com**
Ordering information: Special discounts are available on quantity purchases by corporations, associations, and others.
For details visit **www.BraveSmartandBeautiful.com**.

Brave Smart and Beautiful

Communicating with Teen Daughters

Brave: Having the confidence to try new things, even though she may be scared. Finding the courage to do the right thing.

Smart: Being able to think through situations and make intelligent decisions. Recognize the strength and abilities she brings to the table.

Beautiful: Capturing the spirit from within that allows everyone to see her beauty from the inside out.

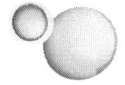

Diane Grant

Table of Contents

Dedication	9
Acknowledgements	11
Preface	15
Introduction	19

Chapter 1
Attitude — 23

Chapter 2
Learning to Listen — 35

Chapter 3
Communication — 41

Chapter 4
Disciplining — 51

Chapter 5
Character Traits to Empower our Developing Daughters — 61

Chapter 6
Independence — 77

Contents Cont'd

Chapter 7
Decision Making Skills   85

Chapter 8
Trust   93

Chapter 9
Motivation   101

Chapter 10
Hygiene and Health   109

Chapter 11
How to Protect Herself   117

Chapter 12
Emotions   125

Chapter 13
Sexual Orientation   131

Thoughts   140

Making Memories Now   143

From the kids   145

Recommended Reading   150

About the Author   151

DEDICATION

To an incredibly strong woman who has left an everlasting mark on my soul.
I was blessed to share such a special bond with her, my Grandma,
Jennie Rizzo Fatone.
She has taught me how to love unconditionally and emulate her warm spirit that lives on through me.
I miss her every day of my life…

Acknowledgements

My children, for their unconditional love.
They have taught me patience and helped me to gain a better understanding of what it means to be a truly supportive Momma.

I am Forever grateful to my amazing children:
Jessica Caputo-Blanc, Douglas Caputo,
Caitlyn Caputo, Kylie Grant, and
Christine Grant-Ligotti, Brian Grant
(my stepchildren). I hold all six of you
so dear to my heart.
Sharing experiences with all of you
has made me the Mom I am today.

Adding to my experience as a Mom
to teen daughters,
Christin Terliesner
(my exchange student daughter from Borken, Germany)
and
Chiara Bruni Zani
(my exchange student daughter from Brescia, Italy)
who have opened their hearts and added
so much joy to all of our lives.

Acknowledgements Cont'd

Thank you Uncle Ralph Fatone, Jr. for stepping in when your brother fell short. Giving me unforgettable childhood memories that allowed me to make sure I made everlasting ones with my children.

I am so fortunate to have an incredible amount of support from so many intelligent, successful women who embraced me with their constructive, caring criticism.

*Ladies in my Lean In group:
*Jennifer Wilson (All About Entertainment)
*Melissa Murck (Melissa Casel Photography)
*Vanessa Valentin (Rising Starz Music Academy)
*Lisa I. Glassman, PA (Real Estate & Estate Planning Attorney)
*Beatrice S. Jacobs, Esq., (Attorney-Family Law)
Margarita Gurri, PhD, CSP (Red Shoe Institute)
for building my confidence in writing and speaking

Aimee Sanchez-Zadak (Professor, Behavioral Strategist)
Angelica Zadak (This is Improv)
Alyiece Moretto (Scenic Designer-Thinking Cap Theatre)
My Aunt, Mary Tweedy (Red-Headed Mary)
Paula Jean Grant
Sarah Sterling
Lauren Smith-Gaines & Susanne Pasqua-Kuligowski
(All of you are my friends for life)

You have encouraged and pushed me at times. Holding me accountable when I needed a gentle shove or encouraging words to move me forward and finish this book.

I Love and Thank all of you!

Mom and Dad
Nancy and John Scollard
I can't thank you enough for always
encouraging my creativty.
For putting together our brood.
Living in our family has made my life so much richer.
Making special rules for me "Because I am Diane"...
Instilling in me a strong work ethic and communication
skills that have always brought me postiive attention.
Daddy, I know you are up above in heaven
smiling at my every move.

Lynn Scollard Junious, My Big Sister, for being my
connection to the world I was cut out of as a young
teenage mother. You kept my spirits up and supported me.
I value our times together.

John Scollard,Jr., Christopher Scollard, Gary Scollard and
Stephen Scollard, my four brothers, partners in crime,
thank you for all the fun memories we share.

Gratitude cannot begin to express
how I feel about this man.
Jim Grant, whom I so proudly call my husband.
You recognized exceptional qualities in me long before
I owned them. As my best friend and love of my life,
I thank you for sharing your life with me,
for loving my children as your own and
encouraging me to be the most amazing me I can be.
For helping me through my fears of success and
for loving the woman I am.

"Many young girls start out with a
twinkle in their eyes and
a fascination about life.
As they mature they are exposed
to many experiences that may seem
of little consequence at the time,
yet can change the direction
of their lives forever."

Diane Grant

PREFACE

How would you like to build a stronger bond and have deep, honest communication with your teen daughter? "Mothers and teen daughters seeing eye to eye," is a phrase not usually said in the same sentence.

Moms, "How many times do we wish we had reacted differently to a situation?" I know I have many times. How can we come up with the Band-Aids that make all our daughters woes feel better? Raising daughters is an awesome responsibility. I consider it to be one of the most rewarding experiences I have ever known. How can we let them know we are always in their corner?

Before reading on, I want every reader to understand, I am not a psychologist and will not ever claim to be one. I have no degree in childrearing. But, I have raised four daughters. This book is my way of sharing some of my thoughts and experiences with you, ones that I found helpful. Moms like me who don't always know the right answer. Moms like me who have learned to trust their gut.

Do you sometimes feel as if you are up against a brick wall with no way of breaking through? Desperately wanting to come up with the words and actions to help your daughter mature into the young lady you know she has the potential to become.

My parenting philosophy has evolved over many years. Initially, I thought strict discipline was the way I should parent. I was raised with this type of discipline. I found it challenging to resist the urge to control.

After a time of feeling discouraged, I rethought my approach. I realized there must be a balance. Parenting with pride and ego was not going to work with any situation. I decided to focus on the end result of what I wanted for my daughter before handing out any punishment.

Each of us has to determine for ourselves what the goals are in raising our teens. I chose to help my daughters become independent, caring, self-respecting, responsible, loving and (most of all) happy.

We all can feel overwhelmed at times, I invite you to read on. My hopes are that you enjoy reading my book, have a few laughs and a few Ah-ha moments. Whatever gems we find that assist in building better communication with our daughters are of value. When our daughters become Mothers of their own daughters, my hope is that some of the experiences and memories they share with us will be what they use as a foundation to build a strong loving bond and relationship with their daughters.

"Don't let life happen to you:
make life happen
because of you."

Anonymous

Introduction

Remember back to a simpler time not so long ago when our daughters slept peacefully in their cribs. We envisioned the incredibly exciting journey that lay ahead, dreaming of long Mother-Daughter talks, and of making wonderful lasting memories together.

"How simple was life back then?" Two A.M. feedings and lack of sleep may have been our biggest concerns.

Now our little princesses have become teenagers, with "attitude," and Eyes-a-Rollin'… Leaving us at times not sure what to do. Torn between when to step in and when to hold back. Let's learn how to develop better communication with them now.

continued

What happened to our independent, sweet, polite, naïve, giggling little girls? They turned into smart-mouthed young ladies with curves and an attitude to boot! Overnight? Not really, they have been evolving. Their personalities and physical development have come very far from the times of peaceful naps in their cribs.

We have an opportunity to greatly influence and empower our teen daughters. How we choose to go about communicating with them now will determine our future relationship with them.

"As soon as I saw you,
I knew an adventure was going to happen."

Winnie the Pooh

CHAPTER ONE

ATTITUDE: The way we greet the day and the people in our lives. Do we think we are better than someone else? Are we critical and judgemental?

It's amazing what happens when we choose to have a positive attitude.
- We are the only ones who can control our mood.
- We must make the shift from being reactive to being proactive.
- Let's guide our daughters to positive thinking

Our Girls can control their future with positive influences and experiences.

What is an attitude, and how does it come into play when helping our daughters?

Facing facts, we all have attitudes, negative and positive ones. Sometimes it's just the tone that we speak with or the mannerisms we use while communicating.

Many of us cannot recognize the negative attitude we convey to others. We are caught up in our own lives. We almost always recognize negative attitudes in other people and often when they are displayed by our teens. Our daughters pick up on many of our attributes, positive and negative ones. All of us are entitled to a bad day every once in a while. But when bad days with negative attitude become a habit, it makes life stressful for everyone around us. Negative attitudes make communication very challenging.

Females, Women, Young Ladies, Mothers and Daughters, however we refer to ourselves… We are an emotional breed. If we weren't we certainly wouldn't be reading this book in hopes of finding a way to better communicate with our daughters. Yes, hormones do play a part, but let's not use that as an excuse for poor behavior.

Helping our daughters recognize that they are in a negative state is not the first step, but close. We can all learn how to communicate using a different, more positive tone, and choosing words that will help us communicate more constructively.

The bullet points below can be helpful in keeping our attitude in check.

- Recognize the negative attitude we are putting out to others.
- Come to terms with the reasons why.
- Take a step back and ask ourselves, "How can I get my point across without being negative or Witchy"?
- Don't make excuses for ourselves.

Many times a negative attitude is in the delivery, the body posture, the tone of voice, the non-sympathetic or non-compassionate way we speak to others. To be truly aware is to put ourselves in the position of the receiving person. Think about how we would feel if someone was speaking to us in the way we are speaking to them. It is a simple concept not easily practiced.

When communicating with our daughters in a controlling tone, it is very difficult to get through to them because they usually shut down. Preaching to them, scolding them will never get our points across. Take a few minutes to step back and think through what we want to communicate, while using a more positive patient attitude. There is more of a chance the outcome will be a less stressful one and better received.

Now we can move towards helping our daughters recognize when they are giving off a bad attitude. Of course if we say it that way, our daughters will become defensive and probably ignore us.

Helping them to understand that no matter how upset or angry they may be, showing a bad attitude is not their most productive option. There are better ways to go about dealing with stressful situations. A suggestion I find helpful is to ask our daughters to take a minute and think things through. Get a handle on what they truly want to communicate. Take the anger out of their communication. By their choice of words or actions, they are the only ones who can control their attitude. Having a negative attitude can shut everyone down and make it much more challenging to get their points across.

When our daughters are left feeling they have nobody to turn to, they may direct their feelings outward towards us with negative or witchy attitudes. They don't want anyone to see their vulnerability. Look for signs that our daughters need help. Sometimes we just need to listen and hear them out. Encourage them to express their feelings and put things in a better perspective. When our daughters are in a stressful situation, often they may show frustration and animosity towards everyone and everything.

Many times the animosity doesn't even make sense. This is a sign they could really use a good ear.

> "When you change the way you look at things, the things you look at change."
>
> Max Planck
> Nobel Prize-winning physicist

The above quote resonates as true. Yet often, so determined to be angry, we may not entertain the idea of changing our attitude when we have a negative one. It's amazing what happens if we choose to have a positive attitude. Let's not give others the power of allowing their negative attitudes to affect us, or blaming them because we are in a negative state. We are the only ones who can control our mood.

We can help our daughters by listening to what the problem or anxiety may be. Often looking at the situation from a different point of view will help them understand things better. Offer insight as to how they would feel if someone showed a negative or nasty attitude towards them. This might encourage all of us to behave better.

Help them to understand that there will be people who may always exhibit a negative attitude. Just because someone acts in a bad way doesn't mean our daughters should act that way too. That would be allowing someone else to determine their mindset. Each of us has control over our behaviors and the kind of attitude we choose to exhibit.

Many times when girls show nasty or negative attitudes, they're reaching out. They may have stresses or things going on in their lives, and may not have anyone to talk to about it. We can help our daughters to understand that sometimes when they are treated mean by other girls, it may have nothing to do with them personally. Teaching our daughters to reach out and show understanding and compassion can be a way to help.

Once we all understand the idea,
that we control our own attitudes,
we will be better able to change our negative
attitudes into more positive ones.

Our daughters see many examples of negative attitudes glorified on T.V., in movies, online and even in books they read. Sometimes, they start to believe that, in order to be popular, they should show a negative or witchy attitude towards others. It's our responsibility as Moms to help them realize that exhibiting this kind of nasty behavior is anything but cool.

It's a reality that often times things aren't going to happen the way they want. Bad things do happen. Sometimes friends aren't really good friends. Pressures with school, grades, teachers, and lack of sleep contribute to people having a bad attitude.

The truth is that having a positive attitude is what will help our daughters get a better perspective on whatever is going on. Positive attitudes will help them become leaders and attract more positive people into their lives. A negative, witchy attitude detracts people, not just friends, but family, teachers, and bosses.

Practice being open-minded and seeing things from their perspective this will genuinely assist in our support of them. They will be more inclined to tell us what is really going on and why they are acting so angry or negative. We need to help them to understand we are not judging and truly want to help them feel better about whatever the issue is.

Sometimes asking our daughters to take a few deep breaths before continuing may be a good idea. It can help to organize their thoughts. When practicing this, it may help them to be in control and not say something they don't mean or may regret.

Try talking when there aren't so many other things going on at the same time. If we are distracted, our daughters may think we don't really care. It is vital that we make them our priority. If we don't give them the time they need with our undivided attention the window of opportunity may pass, making it more difficult to communicate.

It is acceptable to discuss with our daughters that we have noticed some changes in their attitude and that we want to make time to speak with them about it. Make time and be sure they understand that we will be there for them. Do not push it aside, be sure to commit and show them the patience and understanding they deserve.

I like to talk to my daughter when we are out riding bikes or walking. I find she loosens up a little more when she doesn't feel so pressured to speak. Having a relaxed environment helps too. Exercise also tends to help release some tensions, not just for our daughters but for ourselves as well. It allows us to produce the endorphins that help to release some of our stress.

Taking some time to exercise with our daughters is beneficial, and it is doing something with them that benefits both of us. It also gives us some one-on-one time that we both need and keeps our bodies healthier. I genuinely value the times I spend with my daughters. Exercising allows us to connect and free our minds from all the daily pressures that are lurking and can consume so much time in our days.

Thinking back to when my daughter was younger, many nights she would have trouble falling asleep. It took her some time to wind down. After reading her a story or two, I expected that she would fall asleep, "Afterall, that was what bedtime was supposed to be for..." or so I hoped. Walking back into her bedroom fifteen minutes or so later, only to find her wide awake with no intentions of going to sleep. My days usually began at 6am and didn't wind down til around 11pm. As exhausted as I was, I had trouble leaving her alone wide awake. Determined to find a way to do something positive for myself, I made an agreement with her. As long as she promised to relax and rest quietly, I would stay in her room and I would do exercises on the floor. This gave her comfort that I was close by and allowed me to work on relieving some of my stress with yoga, push-ups, and stretches I so desperately needed to help me unwind.

Seeing this as a "Win-Win," I turned it into a nightly ritual, one that I know she fondly remembers.

As she got older and no longer in need of assistance to fall asleep, I continued to exercise in her room and allowed her to count repetitions for me. Many times we would have thoughtful conversations. She loved the company, and I loved that I found time to do something for me without feeling as if I was shorting someone.

I valued that time with her; it was much more memorable than leaving her alone, awake while I watched T.V. or cleaned the house. I believe it also helped my daughter realize that she could count on me. That time of night when my head was clear and I wasn't rushing off to complete another task, helped make me a better listener and better Mother.

It is our responsibility to help guide our daughters to a more positive attitude and outlook. Teaching them to know that they can control their futures by positive influences, positive attitudes, positive decisions, and positive experiences.

"Your attitude is an expression of your values, beliefs and expectations."

Brian Tracy
Author and Motivational Speaker

"Too often we underestimate
the power of
a touch, a smile, a kind word,
a listening ear, an honest compliment,
or the smallest act of caring,
all of which have the potential
to turn a life around."

Leo Buscaglia
Author and Motivational Speaker

Learning To Listen
Chapter Two

LISTENING: Do not judge or overreact; show understanding. Give our daughters our full attention, listen with intention.

Oh, how I couldn't wait until my daughter began to speak. Talking was such a milestone. Wanting her to communicate by saying Mamma, or Dadda. (I'm not sure how prepared I was for the word "NO" shouted at the top of her lungs.) Doing my best to make sure she was fed, bathed, cuddled, loved - these became my goals.

As teens, they still need us almost as much, but in some very different ways. Our daughters develop independence as they mature with many outside influences. It contributes to making them think they don't need us as much as they used to.

Maybe they don't need us to tie their shoes or put ribbons in their hair, but as a Mom we have a significant role and obligation to our daughters. I find it incredibly vital to be in the moment when we are with them. As much as we hear them, how much of the time are we really listening to them?

There are so many distractions on a daily basis that it's truly difficult to listen to every word our daughters have to say. Yet, it is vital for our daughters to know they can share anything with us. Stopping what we feel is a priority, putting it aside and listening, may make all the difference in our relationships with them.

I remember times when I was growing up when
I felt truly alone, as if there wasn't anyone
who cared to listen to me.
Feelings of invisibility and helplessness
as a teenager have taught me
how valuable it is to listen and
be in the moment with my daughters.

I made a list of a few things that I find helpful in developing our strength in listening…

- Be in the moment.

- Make eye contact.
- Put ourselves in our daughter's shoes; understanding where she is coming from will help to put us in the receptive frame of mind.

- Remove all distractions, turning off cell phones, T.V., music, etc.

- Give her all of our undivided attention.

- Schedule a more appropriate time to speak with her depending on what the discussion is about. Do not forget. If a different time is not possible, do our best to clear our minds and open ourselves up to whatever our daughters may want to talk about.

- Do not finish her sentences or make light of her situation. It's better to encourage her with body language by nodding our heads, letting her know we understand and that she has our full attention.

- Keep silent until she is finished or asks you for a reply.

Sometimes, she may not get directly to the point be sure to show her patience. When our daughters do start to talk, we can't feel as if we have to come up with a quick fix for her troubles. The goal is to make her feel comfortable about speaking and opening up to us. Regardless of what the discussion is about, this is practice for all of us. Hopefully we are developing a trust and a strong relationship with our daughter. The goal is for her to feel she can come to us to discuss anything that is on her mind. If we overreact, react negatively or don't truly listen to her, she will probably shut down. If this happens often enough, she will not confide in us at all.

Once the walls go up it is very hard to break through them. It is important not to interrupt. Wait until our daughter is finished and asks for our opinion or thoughts.

> Be sure to put our thoughts together before we speak.

I find it helpful to repeat some of the things she said by rephrasing the issue and encouraging her in a positive way. This is called active listening.

Having our daughter talk through an issue with us out loud helps her to get a better understanding of the problem. The key is to help her move from an emotional response to a more constructive one with a better perspective. Be sure to be alert for things your daughter may not be saying. Look for clues from her body language and facial expressions.

There may be underlying things she may not want to mention, all you can do is assure her that she can tell you anything and that you will be there for her.

Ask her questions that may empower her. Help find a solution or help her come up with an answer that she may not have thought of before.

> How can I be patient when she tells me something I really don't want to hear?

I try to remind myself that 99% of the time the problem is not life or death. 1% of the time it is. If she chooses to come to us for help, be grateful that she has. Taking a deep breath and thinking before speaking will help.

Remember that as a teen she has a lot of emotions, hormones, peer pressures; these can add up and place additional stress on an issue that may be defused simply by having someone to talk to. Let's do our best to make that someone be us.

"I have never come across any Mother who didn't want great communication with their daughters."

Diane Grant

Communication
Chapter Three

COMMUNICATION: A connection between my daughter and myself. It can be verbal or physical. Understanding each other is vital although we may not always agree.

In chapter two we discussed how important it is to be a good listener. Developing strong communication skills that we focus on in this chapter are crucial for all of us and will especially come in handy when raising our daughters. In order for our daughters to become successful in life, it's critical that they are able to articulate and communicate well. As parents, we must encourage our daughters not to be fearful when speaking with adults even though adults can be intimidating at times.

Looking an adult in the eye while communicating her thoughts is a very impressive habit, a habit we should always encourage. It will set them apart in a positive way from other girls. Especially when going to school or to job interviews, using eye-to-eye contact will convey confidence and get the adults' attention as well as making a positive impression.

In order to help develop good communication skills, a great idea is to encourage our daughters to take a J.R.O.T.C. class (Junior Reserve Officer Training Corp) or a debate class in school. Usually the high schools offer both. There are also some leadership classes for teens that can help build confidence and growth in communication as well.

My husband and I encouraged one of our daughters to join the J.R.O.T.C. program in her public middle school and in high school. After looking at the curriculum, we realized it was not necessarily about the military, it was about leadership. J.R.O.T.C. programs teach discipline and positive thinking that every student can benefit from.

No, our daughter was not pressured by the program or by us to go into any of the armed services. She did however develop a great value system, strong work ethic, learned a lot about keeping her body in good physical condition and how to communicate with confidence. It was truly a beneficial program. Her newly developed sense of self after participating in the program really helped her throughout her life with figuring out what was important and how to stay focused on her goals.

Unfortunately, there are some very dangerous people in this world, and we as Moms want to protect our children from them. Often encouraging young children not to talk to strangers. There has to be some kind of middle ground. Otherwise we will create anti-social, paranoid daughters with this kind of thinking. We have to be able to communicate with all people, ones we know as well as those we don't.

Words are not the only way we communicate. Our facial expressions are one way of communicating without saying any words. It's challenging for me to keep my facial expressions from giving away my thoughts, especially when I do not like what I am hearing. It's good to practice processing the situation before reacting, either with words or facial gestures. At times my expressions are not received the way I mean them to be. This is something that I still have trouble with.

The affections I show with all of my daughters has always come naturally, although verbal communication at times has been difficult. I didn't always know how to communicate my thoughts without my emotions getting in the way. I find it helpful to think things through before reacting. Communicating is sometimes challenging, but it is well worth the effort.

Asking questions that will prompt conversation may be a way of getting our daughters to share their feelings. How we phrase our words can assist in breaking down the barriers our daughters sometimes put up. Asking questions that aren't easily answered with one word answers like, "How was your day?" instead "What did you like best about your day?" Many times we are so eager to hear about their day or about their plans that we push too hard. I don't think it is intentional because we want to be informed. Probably one of the surest ways to have our daughters shut down and tune out is to push too hard.

Think in advance about what words we can use to help our daughters convey their feelings or thoughts. Remember being a good listener is a valuable characteristic we need to practice. Sometimes our daughters may need some quiet time to relax and unwind after a long day. Don't think because they don't want to talk that it has something to do with us. Suggest that they tell us they need some quiet time and will talk with us later. We don't want her to feel as if we are bombarding her, or leave us feeling as though she wants to shut us out.

I picked up my daughter from middle school one afternoon. As soon as she got into the car I could see on her face that she was distraught about something.

Steam was seeping out of her ears and she looked like she was about to explode. I hadn't had much luck in the past trying to get her to openup when she was this upset, so I decided to take a deep breath myself and wait it out until she was ready to talk. After ten minutes or so, my daughter was able to tell me everything that had happened and how terribly she was bullied throughout that day. Her spirit was crushed. I did my best not to overreact, though it was extremely difficult. I knew that if she sensed how angry I was at these girls, it would make her feel even more deflated.

Sometimes it's better to just listen and not react. Reacting out of anger or hurt can truly make the incident more stressful and painful for our daughters. As many of us have experienced in our past, some girls can be jealous, mean, domineering, and sometimes downright awful.

On the flip side, girls can also be very supportive of one another, by coming to each other's aid and truly being a great friend. Sometimes just being there and letting our daughters vent without making judgments is the best way to handle these kind of situations.

Although, there are some times when interference is needed, trust your gut on how to handle each specific situation. If our daughter decides not to share with us what is troubling her, we cannot force the issue. We can communicate to her that when she is ready to share, we will be there to listen. Usually our daughters will let us know if they need us to go to their defense. One of the goals in communicating with our daughters is to let them know there isn't anything they cannot tell us. We will not judge her, only help guide her to better decisions, offering understanding and insight.

For our own sanity, when there is a situation that is stressful and turns into a screaming match, take a step back and regroup. It will not be easy, but once we get control of ourselves, our daughters will not be able to feed off of our anger. Be firm and communicate that when she is ready to speak civilly, then we will be able to continue the discussion.

We can always suggest a "Do Over." It is when one or both of us has said something that we regret or with an attitude that is "less than lovely!", (as my dear friend Margarita Gurri, Phd., CSP says).

Apologizing and asking for a "Do Over" can help us both understand that in the heat of the moment, in which things are said that aren't always meant in the tone we deliver them in.

Communication and listening skills go hand in hand. Our daughters deal with many stressful situations throughout their teenage lives, and it helps that we can listen and understand them.

There could be times when our support and understanding will not be enough. Our daughters have many challenges and some that may require outside assistance.

Our daughters may need a professional, maybe a physician, a psychologist, a teacher or a counselor who will have a lot more experience and knowledge then we as Moms have. These individuals can help our daughters and ourselves cope with certain situations along with the emotional highs and lows they may experience.

> Please, we cannot sell this idea short.
> We have to listen to our gut.
> God gave us instinct, it is powerful.
> If something doesn't seem right,
> it probably isn't.

Sometimes, something may be happening, and our daughters are too embarrassed to talk to us about it. Remember their minds are still developing and sometimes they may not be sure how to cope with some of these stressful situations and all of the emotions that go along with them. Don't ignore the signs that our daughters may be reaching out to us for help.

On the other hand, we have to recognize, that our daughters may just be having an off day. They may be reacting too sensitively. There is a fine line and it will not be easy to decipher. All we can do as Moms is do the best that we can and listen to our gut.

When I was a preteen, I was experiencing a lot of headaches. After seeing the pediatrician and ophthalmologist it was decided that I should see a counselor for help. Unfortunately, I saw a very inexperienced psychologist who didn't really know what to do with me. After weeks of her not getting through to me, I pleaded with my parents to let me stop going. The truth was I really did need to speak to someone.

This psychologist had no clue how to reach me. I had been sexually molested, and I needed help. Convincing myself that I could handle this situation on my own, I chose not to mention it during my counseling sessions, unless she out and out asked me if I was being molested. I obviously didn't know how to help myself.

Needless to say my psychologist never asked. I never shared and I continued to make poor decisions in my teenage years and into my adulthood. I was ashamed as if the molestation was my fault. I continued to put aside what had happened to me. It took many years before I was ready to reach out for counseling, when I was in my 30's. I went to speak with a psychologist and she helped me tremendously, I forgave myself and no longer had shame or guilt.

Be sure to ask the right questions. Sometimes teens are too embarrassed or they want to push it to the background in hopes it will go away. A question as simple as: "Has anyone ever touched you or done something to you that you were uncomfortable with and were afraid to tell me?" Comminicate with our daughters that there isn't anything they cannot tell us.

> I invite you to share my story with your daughters in hopes they see how poor decisions can snowball and affect them throughout their lives. Make sure you are the kind of Mom who is receptive to whatever she needs to share.

"Do not train a child to learn
by force or harshness;
but direct them to it
by what amuses their minds,
so that you may be better able
to discover with accuracy
the peculiar bent of the genius of each."

Plato
Ancient Greek Philosopher and Author

CHAPTER FOUR

DISCIPLINING: The practice of training others to obey rules or developing a code of behavior. Using corrective tools when our daughters don't follow the rules.

We are hurting our daughters if we don't think disciplining is our responsibility. Expecting the school to take on this responsibility is ridiculous. If we don't do it, our daughters will be unprepared in many aspects of their lives. "I think we owe it to them, don't you?"

Discipline is carrying out a punishment or correction in our daughters behavior if she does not follow the rules we have set.

I have made many mistakes trying to instill discipline by carrying out punishment when warranted with my children. My upbringing consisted of getting screamed at a lot, cursed at, and being grounded. I started this kind of disciplining with my own children thinking this is what was expected of me to raise a responsible child.

Needless to say it didn't work. It left me feeing angry, stressed and guilty about how I handled each situation. Because this was the disciplining I was raised with, I often felt like a failure that my children didn't behave the way I expected them to.

All the screaming did was make them feel worthless, and I soon joined them in feeling that way, too. I had not realized the importance of understanding that a mistake was made, and learning from that mistake is more valuable than remembering the punishment that was attached to it.

None of us likes to be told what to do. As a Mom this leaves us in a challenging position. Balancing guidance, authority, love, and being consistent all at the same time. - "Yikes!" I'm grateful I learned to take a step back and figure out I had to do things differently. I asked myself what the real goal was.

> Understanding the importance of learning a lesson and helping my children understand they could learn from their mistakes became my goal in carrying out discipline.

It's crucial to discuss the rules or Code of Behavior that is expected of them, making sure it's clear. There should be no misunderstandings. Our daughters must know what is expected of them.

> I find it helpful to separate "My Rules" into two categories, "Hard Rules" and "Soft Rules." Everything is not black and white, there is grey. In some instances grey will apply.

My definition of "Hard Rules", these are rules that are ALWAYS expected to be followed, some examples are:

- Don't smoke or use drugs

- No underage drinking

- Always be truthful about where you are

- Respect yourself and others

After determining what the guidelines will be, communicate with our daughters so they can understand what the rules are and why we feel these rules are important. Also convey to them that these rules are to be followed. As Moms we cannot feel as if we are being mean or unfair. This code of behavior will help our daughters throughout their lives. Teenagers need responsibilities and rules, even if they fight us on them.

I'm sure many of us have heard "Mom, but Ashley's mom is letting her go." I found it difficult sometimes, but we have to be strong enough to say "I am not Ashley's Mom, I'm your Mom and you are not going."

I was convinced my parents didn't want me to have any fun while I was a teenager. I was very wrong. They wanted to insure my safety.

I know now they had good reasons behind many of their rules. Living by the code of behaviors they set created many positive attributes that have served me well in my teenage and adult life.

A few notes I found helpful when disciplining my daughters:

- Don't punish under stress.
  No matter how bad the situation is, take some deep breaths. 99% of the problems are able to be corrected. 1% are devastating, possibly life threatening. Understand what kind of situation we are dealing with. Taking a few breaths usually enables us to take a minute before reacting and put things in the proper perspective.

- Take a step back to process the situation.

- Remember, "We are parents, not friends."

- Our daughters are not bad, but they made a bad decision.

My "Soft Rules" are rules such as curfew, bedtimes, chores. The soft rules are not negotiable, but I can allow some modifications when I determine it is warranted. Not when she thinks it should be applied.

～

We can't say no to everything.

This is where my definition of "Soft Rules," comes into play. Sometimes punishment is not warranted. Thinking things through helps me to make a better decision and to choose wisely. No matter what our daughters tell us, we cannot overreact. Otherwise, the wall may go up, and we will lose our ability to get through to them. There are lessons our daughters can learn when they make a bad choice. I find learning the lesson alone can sometimes be punishment enough. It's vital to keep an open mind.

I've seen some Moms who think it's the schools responsibility to discipline their daughters. Moms who don't want to seem mean or uncool. I see discipline as a tool to help guide our daughters into making better decisions and helping to prepare them for life.

Being consistent is one of the most valuable things I want to share. Our daughters need us to be consistent with the "Hard Rules" they need to know where they stand and where we stand as their Mom. We are not here to be her friend. We are here to be her Mother. Paying attention to what our daughters are doing, who they hang around with, where they are, and what kind of decision making skills they have practiced will benefit all of us.

As teenagers our daughters aren't always the best judges of what the right thing is to do. The development of the frontal lobe (part of the brain where caution is developed) isn't fully matured. It is our job to give them the tools and be there along the way to help guide them into becoming incredible young ladies. We should not turn the other way because we don't really want to see what our daughters are doing. We have to take responsibility and see that our daughter understands when she has done something wrong.

In advance we may want to think through some options that can be used as a consequence when the situation arises. Being clear with "Hard Rules" really helped me with disciplining my daughter. I didn't want to have too many Hard Rules. I chose the ones I feel strongly about and always enforce them.

Understanding that we as Moms, do not want to create droids as daughters, we have to pick our battles. Teenagers do need to have some slack with "Soft Rules". We need to take into consideration the stress they are under daily between peer-pressure, lack of sleep, pressures to do well in school, hormones and some obstacles of which we are not even aware. Rules like bedtimes, or events on school nights, are some soft rules that I have bent on occasion.

Sometimes I would let my daughter stay home from school, sort of a Mother-Daughter Day Off. We would spend the day together doing something unexpected and fun. It helped her to recharge her batteries and not take herself and life too seriously. Looking back, those are some of the most memorable days we both treasure.

Discipline is never easy, but making a plan in advance helped me be better prepared, so I didn't over punish or under punish. Choosing the right time to administer consequences was not easy. Remembering to have a clear mind when disciplining will always benefit the situation. Be sure to defuse the emotions in ourselves before discussing the punishment.

It's vital to remember that we should point out their good behavior, too. When thinking about disciplining, punishment usually comes to mind. Although we can't ignore commending our daughters for good behavior. It's difficult to take notice of all of the good things they do. The wrong things often take presidence.

Giving credit when we see our daughters study hard and do well on a test, or do the dishes without being asked, these are situations when we should thank them. It's a perfect opportunity to let them know we notice the good stuff too. Mentioning the good behavior will help them to accept when they get disciplined for bad behavior.

> Believe it, our daughters
> will respect us for having rules.
> They may not admit it now
> but when they mature
> they will understand
> the rules we made
> were made out of love for them.

"It is character that got us out of bed,
commitment that moved us into action
and discipline that
enabled us to follow through."

Zig Ziglar
Author and Motivational Speaker

Character Traits to Empower our Developing Daughters
Chapter Five

CHARACTER TRAITS: are all aspects of a person's behavior and attitudes that make up that person's personality.

Some Positive Character Traits

- Respect
- Integrity
- Compassion
- Honesty
- Responsibility

There are many positive character traits worthy of developing. The character we display shows the world who we are. Having good character will set them apart from other teens and be beneficial in our daughters' futures.

How can we cultivate positive character traits when on a daily basis our daughters are exposed to so many examples of poor values and weak character?

I found it helpful to remember that from a very young age my daughters were watching me all the time. They witnessed first-hand how I treated others and how I reacted to situations that were professional, stressful, challenging, or happy.

"You must begin to think of yourself
as becoming the person
you want to be."

David Viscott
Radio Personality

Understanding the impact I have on my daughters led me to ask myself these valuable questions

Are WE compassionate towards others?

Do WE treat ourselves and others with respect?

Are WE honest?

Do WE value ourselves and others?

Are WE prejudiced?

Do WE take responsibility for our actions?

Are WE so wrapped up with ourselves that we do not reach out to a friend who is in need?

Do WE think winning is most important?

Do WE show patience towards others?

> Being a Positive Role Model and leading by example is an ideal way to help our daughters learn without having to lecture them.

RESPECT...

A way of thinking or showing admiration for something or someone that is good, valuable, important, elicited by their qualities or achievements.

Helping our daughters to understand that showing respect for others is key to their earning others' respect.

Our daughters attitude and actions towards others should be respectful, and most especially towards us. I know it's a challenge to constantly be on top of our daughters' behavior. It is necessary. If we don't pay attention and tune in to the way they speak to us and others, their disrespect may become a habit and could result in a constant delivery of disrespect that as Moms we may unfortunately become immune to.

It's vital that our daughters know what is expected of them. It's never too late to start. If we think new rules have to be set, then find a time when emotions are calm. Explain the new rules. Discuss how we don't approve of the disrespectful ways they have been acting or speaking to us. We may not have pointed it out in the past or knew how to correct it, but it's about time and there need to be some changes made. Let them know we expect to be talked to in a respectful way. From now on we will immediately bring the disrespectful behavior to their attention.

It's up to us to decide on what the repercussions will be when our daughters talk or act disrespectfully towards us. There should be zero tolerance.

As time goes by with us bringing it to their attention it should lesson the disrespectful behavior. Be sure not to lose our cool and become enraged or disrespectful ourselves.

Although it may be frustrating at times, it will teach our daughters to respect others and in turn help them develop rules for themselves as to how they will allow others to treat them.

A successful future rides heavily
on how our daughters treat themselves
and other people.

Our daughters must learn to love and value (respect) themselves. If they don't value themselves it will be hard for others to value them.

Dealing with a boy's attention will not be easy. We must help our daughters to realize how exceptional they are and not every boy that is attracted to them is going to be "Exceptional" or "The Right One."

It's an awesome feeling to have someone be attracted to you or like you. Blinded by the attention, it's hard to see the other person may not have your best interest in mind.

When I was a teen I saw myself only through the eyes of others. I measured myself especially by how the boys saw and treated me. Depending on how the boys felt about me was how I felt about myself. If the boys thought I was pretty then, I must be pretty; if the boys thought I was not, I must not be. This couldn't have been farther from the truth. My self-esteem was ridiculously low.

I didn't know how to show respect or love for myself. This lesson took many years for me to learn. I had to become secure and happy with myself and not depend on someone else to validate me. Finding confidence and self-respect was a worthwhile struggle.

Developing good values and positive
character traits is a compass
to which our daughters can hold true.
It is essential that our daughters
value themselves as well as others.

"Integrity without knowledge is weak and useless, and knowledge without integrity is dangerous and dreadful."

Samuel Johnson
English Writer

INTEGRITY...

A practice of doing the right thing. Having strong convictions and being able to stand by them.

Encourage our daughters to develop a belief system based on knowledge, honesty, and accountability. Helping our daughters to understand that making the choice between right from wrong may be easier than holding firm with their decision when challenged by their peers.

We are not perfect. There is good and bad in each of us. It's often difficult to do the right thing vs. ignoring a situation or going along with the crowd. Being strong and committed to act on what she knows is right will create a leader. She will become a person others will strive to be like.

Will our daughters be the ones to stand up for someone who is being bullied or the girl who will stand by in silence watching, or worse, participate in the bullying? It's critical to help our daughters figure out where they will stand. Discussing scenarios, acting out, or brainstorming, may help our daughters to think about how they will react, and what they will say, hopefully before they experience a challenging situation like bullying.

Assure our daughters that just because they didn't take a stand in one instance, doesn't mean they can't take a positive stand in the future. Open discussions about how she may react if put into particular situations can help her put things in a better perspective.

Ask our daughters to think about the kind of person she wants to be. Discuss what she considers positive character traits. Helping her to understand the meaning of Integrity.

- Encourage her to be kind to others.
- Show respectful behavior towards herself and to others.
- Point out when we see our daughters exhibiting an action that shows good values or positive character.
- Keep an open mind when our daughters bring up their own experiences or dilemmas.

Encouraging our daughters to ask better questions of themselves in any situation is an opportunity to help them think things through. Sometimes our daughters may not verbalize their answers, but seeds of thought will be planted and hopefully guide them into making better decisions and actions later.

Some examples that may start the conversation:

- How will she handle a bullying situation? What if she was witnessing a bully picking on another person?

- Does she think it's OK to accept another "More Popular" girls party invite if she has already rsvp'd to a different friend?

- How does she feel if she did something wrong, and no one finds out about it; is it still wrong?

COMPASSION...

Showing sympathy towards someone else who is in distress and having the desire to alleviate and help them through the pain. The act or capacity for sharing the painful feelings of another.

Compassion plays a crucial role in happiness. Developing compassion within ourselves and others can help establish a path to consciousness that many don't ever practice or understand.

With all of the strife and cruelty in this world Mothers have the opportunity to welcome and encourage compassion every day.

Be aware and show our daughters examples of compassion towards ourselves and others.

Ask our daughters to visualize a friend who is having a really rough time. To think about what she may do to help her friend, to come up with ways not necessarily to fix the friends trouble but develop listening skills and suggestions of how she can help her friend look at the problem from a different perspective. This is an example of practicing compassion.

Everyone goes through hard times. How we deal with them and how we support others in a positive caring way shows true compassion.

HONESTY...

The quality or fact of being honest, truthful, and sincere.

Honesty is developed from a young age. If we put tremendous fear into our daughters about lying, they may be afraid to tell the truth if it will get them into trouble.

I would much rather my girls be truthful than feel they have to lie as to not disappoint me. I rely on good communication, and I have had discussions that if they are not being honest with me and I find out, they will be in more trouble than if they own up and tell me the truth.

Our daughters know right from wrong, we all do. Convincing our daughters to always do what is right can be a challenge, but honesty is always the best decision. There is a lot of pressure on teens to make the right choices. Being true to herself is vital and will serve her well.

It's our responsibility to let our daughters know that it's OK to be different and not go along with what her friends may be doing. Using her conscience as her guide will be a great benefit. I count on my daughters to be honest and take them at their word.

Ultimately, being honest is what I want them to expect from themselves. We can't be with them all the time. It's their responsiblilty to take ownership and be honest and truthful to themselves and others.

"Honesty and Integrity
are absolutely
essential for success in life,
all areas in life.
The good news is that anyone
can develop both
Honesty and Integrity."

Zig Ziglar
Author, Salesman and Motivational Speaker

RESPONSIBILITY...

An act of being responsible for something or someone, a duty, a job.

Being responsible genuinely helps our daughters develop a direction for their future. Teens who have had responsibilities while growing up understand that they have to contribute in order to make their lives more meaningful.

Responsibility can start with simple things that our daughters have to do in order to contribute to the family. They can help care for a younger sibling, or help younger siblings with homework. Laundry is an important chore that will help when they are on their own or away at college. It's not only chores that help develop responsiblilties.

Encourage volunteering with them at school or through service clubs. Volunteering at a soup kitchen, can help our daughters understand there are many less fortunate people in this world, and it is an awesome opportunity to practice many of the key character traits they are striving to embody.

Developing positive self-worth and responsibility can lead to leadership qualities that will greatly benefit our daughters in their future.

We know our daughters see a lot of negative actions in their everyday lives. Our responsibility as Moms is to assist our daughters into becoming "Good People." Positive, responsible, ready to face the world with a set of core values that show what incredible ladies they are. Armed with these character traits, when practiced, will become part of who they truly are, and will lead them to a successful, happy life.

"Accept responsibility for your life.
Know that it is you who will get you where you want to go, no one else."

Les Brown
Motivational Speaker and Author

"It is not what you do for your children
but what you have taught them
to do for themselves,
that will make them
successful human beings."

Ann Landers
Advice Columnist

Independence
Chapter Six

INDEPENDENCE: freedom from outside control or support; making decisions on their own. a state of being independent.

I found it difficult balancing between knowing when to hold back and when to let them go. I wanted to see my daughters succeed and experience all of life's amazing treasures. Yet, I wanted to protect them and keep them out of harm's way.

It's a struggle between wanting to protect our daughters, keeping them from experiencing any pain or disappointment and letting them go to experience independence and the awesome things life has to offer.

I made a big mistake years ago, subconsciously thinking my daughters somehow needed more protection than my sons. This is a feeling I needed to keep under wraps, if I wanted to help my daughters to excel and develop into strong confident women. I knew I couldn't coddle them or be overprotective.

> It's crucial that we don't always prevent them from falling.
> If we do
> they will not know how to get up after they do inevitably fall.

We've all at one point in our lives had to figure things out for ourselves. Although we answer to many different people throughout our lives (parents, teachers, bosses) it's vital to learn how to make decisions. Decisions that we choose, based on how we feel, not based on what others want us to think and feel. We have to be comfortable with developing independent thoughts and being able to voice them.

I wanted to encourage "out of the box" thinking as well. I know I don't want to raise droids or followers. Wanting my daughters to make valuable contributions and be independent, forward thinking young ladies is an opinion I always felt strongly about. It was challenging at times but well worth every effort.

Of course when they were little it was our responsiblity to protect them. But if they haven't experienced disappointment as teenagers they will not know how to cope when something doesn't go their way as adults. Helping our daughters become well equipped to handle the pressures that life has in store for them is instrumental to their growth, as is helping them to understand they have the ability within themselves to face many challenges in their future.

The trust our daughters have earned will help determine how much independence they're ready for.

Whenever our daughters experience accomplishments, no matter how small, it will build their self-confidence. The more confident they become, the more they will challenge themselves to try new things.

Overcoming challenges helps them practice on making good decisions, developing confidence and independent thought.

As a young girl, I can remember my Mom allowing me to bake my first cake. I must have been 4 or 5 and with my Mom's help, I was able to measure out the ingredients and mix it. I needed some help with the oven, of course. But, once the cake was finished I was so proud of myself, I wanted to share it with the world. I decided to share it with my neighbor, an elderly woman who didn't smile very much. I will never forget her smile that day when I presented her with a piece of my surprise cake.

I'm not quite sure if my Mom ever knew what a positive impact this made on me and how proud I was of myself. I think she was just trying to keep me busy, but it was a great idea, one I have shared with my daughters, and granddaughters as well. Having our daughters share their success is a tremendous confidence booster. This experience added a jump-start to my independence.

> We are doing our daughters a disservice if we don't put aside our "Over Protective, Controlling Feelings", and teach them how to be independent, strong, and capable to stand up for themselves.

Let's encourage our daughters not to be afraid to try new things or to venture out and meet new or different people. The more opportunities presented will contribute significantly to their self-confidence and independence.

It was a simpler life when I was growing up in the 70's; there were earlier opportunities to go to the corner store to buy milk or bread contributing to my independence. My friend and I would also ride our bikes miles away from our homes by ourselves as long as we were home by dinnertime. I doubt our parents had any idea how far we would ride.

These days it will be a little more challenging to set up ways for our daughters to become independent of us. Unfortunately, society has become more dangerous and in many areas not such a good idea to send them off to the corner store.

We have to be creative when trying to have our daughters experience something that will build their independence. It can be done. Make a conscious effort to figure out a way. Having a good sense of independence is a strong attribute from which all our teens can benefit.

Awhile back, one of my daughters wanted to go to the beach with her friends for the day. She had just turned thirteen and some of her friends parents had dropped their daughters at the beach earlier that morning and weren't going to pick them up until later in the afternoon. My daughter thought it was perfectly OK for me to drop her at the beach as well. I didn't agree. My daughter thought I was being untrusting and that I didn't think she could handle herself. That was not the case, I knew they should not be alone all day. I agreed to take her to meet her friends and told her I would sit far enough away that she could feel independent of me but close enough if she needed me I would be there.

Much to her surprise they did need me. The lifeguard saw the girls alone and when there was an issue with the girls and riptides in the water, he asked where their parents were. The lifeguard was pretty surprised to hear most of them did not have a parent with them. I know my daughter felt better that she could answer the lifeguard that her mom was over there.

> We also have to be careful with how we let our daughters experience independence.
> Their age and maturity should dictate your decisions.

> As a Mom trust your gut.
> You be the judge with what
> you will allow your daughter to do.
> Don't let another parent dictate for you.

∽

If we fail to raise a daughter who is independent of us, think about what may lie ahead for her... What if our daughters are afraid to speak their minds, become followers, instead of becoming a leader... or if we have coddled, spoiled and over-protected our daughters too much, they may think every small disappointment is devastating.

We cannot and will not always be there to protect them and pick up the pieces. They are so much stronger than many give them credit for. Communicate with our daughters letting them understand there isn't anything they can't accomplish, as long as they set their minds to it, and are willing to take the proper steps.

"Everything in life happens for a
good reason.
It teaches you something.
Treat every mistake you make as a lesson
to make you a better person."

Author Unknown

Decision Making Skills
Chapter Seven

DECISION MAKING: Developing the mindset to think through and make the best choice.

    As a teen learning to make a decision with limited experience and knowledge can be overwhelming. Understanding everything isn't always black and white may be a lesson in and of itself.

    Good decision making skills develop over time. The more information and experience we have, usually the better decisions we can make.

> "Sometimes a decision you make will be inconsequential, and sometimes it will affect you for the rest of your life…"

There are many difficult decisions our teens are faced with today. Peer pressures are heightened, drugs are easy to get, alcohol is advertised as a cool way to unwind, the internet allows instant gratification and ways to communicate that weren't around when I was growing up. But, whether or not to have sex has been an issue forever. The ages of kids having sex is significantly younger and has become more riskier than ever. With AIDS, HIV, STD's, Pregnancies are some of the many reasons not to have sex as a teen. Our teens are not prepared emotionally and aren't mature enough to take proper precautions. Having sex as a teenager, may lead to danger and life-altering outcomes that can change the direction of their future in a negative way forever.

I was a teen pregnancy statistic. Yes, I got pregnant at 17. It wasn't that I purposefully got pregnant. I thought, as many teens do, "It will never happen to me." Boy, was I wrong.

I gave birth to my first daughter, Jessica, just two weeks after I turned 18, because I didn't respect myself, or truly love myself, thinking sex = love. I had sex way too early, and found myself in a situation where I had to choose... my future as I had originally planned or the choice to be a teen mother. A decision not easily made at seventeen.

Working diligently to make the right decisions from that point on for my daughter became my focus. I fumbled with self-esteem and self-love issues for a time. Life was hard, strongly due to my lack of life experiences and self-respect. I learned how to trust my gut with child rearing. My gut served me well.

Many decisions our daughters will have to make are not life or death. Many times there are some choices that cannot be taken back and some of those can pose a great risk.

Some examples of these bad decisions that can forever change our daughters lives and the lives of others:

- Texting while driving.
- Getting into a car when the driver is under the influence of drugs or alchohol.
- Reckless driving.
- Having sex too early and unprotected sex.

These are a few examples where bad choices can lead to terrible outcomes.

A number of years ago I lived in a quaint little bedroom community, where everyone thought nothing bad happens here. In the middle of the night a couple of 14-year-old boys decided to take their parents car out for a short ride in their neighborhood. The boys woke up another friend who lived down the street to join them along with his younger brother who was 11. All 4 boys decided to include 2 girls who also lived in the neighborhood. Showing off for the girls the driver drove around a bend at about 80 miles an hour and struck a tree head on.

The driver who was one of only two wearing his seatbelt, walked away with a few bruises. The girls were thrown from the car and both died in the arms of the police officers on the scene. The brothers died within a few weeks after the accident, the passenger boy who was 14 and wearing his seatbelt, spent 3 months in the hospital, with a crushed pelvis and numerous other injuries. I believe the 14-year-old driver was convicted of vehicular manslaughter and spent many years in jail to think about his foolish actions. One family lost both of their sons. Everyone lost their innocence for a stupid immature decision.

> It's our job to help our daughters make better choices. This is a perfect example that sometimes a poor decision will affect you and others for the rest of your life.

Keeping our daughters naïve is not the best recommendation. Although, trying to prevent them from being neurotic is also challenging. There is a happy medium that you will be able to find.

Many teenager minds are not able to think through some of their actions. As Moms, we have to be aware that they will not always make the best decisions. Keeping open communication with them is crucial even though it can be challenging at times.

Ideas that you may find helpful:
(some of these suggestions apply to older teens)

- Anytime they go out with their friends, I ask that they text me when they arrive. If they leave to go somewhere other than where their original destination is, they are to text me as well.

- When they go out on a date, the boy is to come to the door and meet either myself or my husband first. Be sure to make note of what he looks like, what kind of car he is driving. It may sound neurotic but if she doesn't come home you have a place to start. Be open with your daughter explaining that this is for her own safety. If she doesn't understand, then maybe she is with the wrong guy, or isn't mature enough to go out on dates.

- I also have an agreement with my daughters that if they are in a situation where they do not feel comfortable, they can call me and I will pick them up, whatever the time and wherever they are. If they were drinking or doing something I would not approve of, I will not make immediate judgments but, they have to be willing to discuss it. They will be in a lot less trouble if they called me, than if they had stayed and did not call for me. The most important thing is that they are safe and that they know my love for them is unconditional.

Think about how you would feel if you received a phone call late at night and was told that your child was in an accident? I have never received that kind of call. Although one night, I did receive a phone call from a police officer telling me that the boy who was driving my daughter (17 years old) home from a date was driving in excess speeds of 90 miles per hour on a back road. I couldn't thank the officer enough for telling me. As a father himself he thought I should know how this boy had showed no regard for my daughters safety. I was able to help my daughter come to the decision that this boy was not the one for her.

I've sat through a number of seminars and read articles about the frontal lobe of the teenagers brain and how in many cases it isn't fully developed until their early twenties. This is the part of the brain where caution is developed. After hearing this the first time, it was like a bell went off in my head. It now made sense why so many teens (I was one of them) thought they were invincible. "Nothing bad would ever happen to them." I wish many of the teens I knew were still around to understand how very risky their actions were. Unfortunately, a number of them are no longer here because of the poor decisions they made and paid for these bad decisions with their lives.

Don't let our daughters be a statistic. Starting these conversations about good decisions as soon as possible will help them develop a better judgment and hopefully prevent horrible consequences.

"All the world is made of faith, and trust, and pixie dust."

J.M. Barrie
Author of Peter Pan

Chapter Eight

TRUST: Knowing you can count on someone, believing in them. Giving our daughters chances, choices, responsibilities, opportunities to show they can be trusted. Above all, being the Mom they can depend on.

Building trust starts at a young age. Ever have a child throw their bottle on the floor while they sat in the highchair, time after time? They were testing us to see if they can count on us to be there and pick it up. At a very early age children start to determine who it is they can trust. Of course our daughters' needs change as they mature. They still need to know that they can count on us to be there for them.

Many teens have shared that they feel their parents don't understand them and can't relate to them. I know I have felt a disconnect with my daughters at times.

Listening, being interested in them, spending quality time with our daughters play a big part in building trust. Trust is given when there is honesty.

There are times when we know something is truly bothering our daughters, but they don't want to or know how to confide in us. Hounding them or prodding for information, doesn't usually work. We can only hope our daughters will eventually share what their troubles are. They are torn between telling us something we would want to know, and being assured that we won't go off the deep end if they tell us something that we wouldn't approve of.

Trust is vital to have in our relationships with our daughters. If they feel they cannot come to us, they will go to someone else or keep it inside. Holding their feelings in has its own set of strains for them to endure. Practice being there but waiting patiently for the time our daughters are ready to share.

With that being said, it's imperative that at times we give them some space. There is a balance we have to find and it may be different for each of us. Please, resist the temptation to hover or over-control. Our daughters need to develop independently from us. We have to allow them to venture out and experience the world. It's inevitable that they will keep some things private.

Let's agree not to read our daughters diaries. Depending on their age, I do recommend visiting their facebook, email and instagram accounts from time to time. Discussing with them, that as a parent it's our responsibility to check in and see what they're up to. There is a fine line between being nosey and being informed.

It took a long time before I would allow my daughter to have a Facebook and Instagram account. Of course she was not happy with my decision I explained to her that social media is a very powerful tool, and it was not that I didn't trust her or that I didn't think she was too immature for this responsibility. Some of the teens she was friends with were not kids who had a good grasp of how much damage can be done to a persons reputation using social media. When girls are mad at each other or jealous or just think they're playing a joke on someone, they can post harsh words or inappropriate photos that cannot be taken back, once posted it is out in public for everyone to see, regardless of the safety precautions that can be set on her account.

> There have been too many suicides from teens who have had their reputations ruined on social media. Don't be afraid to have these discussions. It may save their lives or someone else's.

We don't have to know every detail of our daughters' lives, but we should have a good idea of who her friends are, what they're doing and where they spend their time. Just because they may be able to drive doesn't mean we give up the responsibility to steer them in the right direction.

I let my daughters know that they have my trust until they do something to break it. They are informed of the rules, including basic ones that have to do with their safety and common sense, like "No Drinking," "No Smoking," "No Drugs," etc. There may be times when they break the rules. Even if they don't get caught, it's still wrong. They must understand that they've broken our trust.

Trust is something that has to be nurtured and respected. It's their responsibility to think things through before they act.

What to do when the trust has been broken?

- The most important thing is to not let our emotions rule our reactions.

- Take some deep breaths and allow some of the steam to dissipate prior to discussing what has happened.

- It's vital to let our daughters know we are disappointed and that she has done something to lose our trust.

- Our trust is something she can earn back in time.

    She may have made a bad decision but we still love her. Take some time to discuss the situation, helping her to understand she is responsible for her actions.

    Taking responsibility is crucial in earning back our trust. Guide her to positive thinking and better decisions. Remember we're not her friend, we are her parent. Don't feel guilty about punishing her if she's broken the rules. Going overboard with a heavy punishment may feel right at the time, but not the best decision. Be sure the punishment fits the crime. Our main goal should be to make sure she understands what she has done wrong and she needs to make better choices in the future. (Refer to Chapter 4 on Discipline)

We have to allow opportunites for our daughters to earn back our trust. Start with small steps first, then larger steps. Giving her more privileges as she shows us that she can be trusted again.

Start conversations with her on how we feel about her breaking our trust. Ask her to share what ideas she has to earn back our trust. Open communication is crucial in getting insight as to why she made the bad decisions that led to her losing our trust.

> Trust is a gift to be cherished,
> it may be challenged along the way,
> learn to forgive and build again.

Trust is the glue that holds a relationship together.

> Don't let life happen to you,
> make life happen because of you.

"What would you do if you weren't afraid."

Sheryl Sandberg
COO of Facebook and Author

Chapter Nine

MOTIVATION: stimulate someone into striving for a goal, using ambition, initiative, drive and determination.

How can we motivate our teenage daughters into doing their homework, chores, getting a part-time job? When our daughters were younger it was fairly easy to motivate them. Many times they needed a reward of some kind in order to do what we wanted them to. Sometimes it was just the act of doing something for us that was enough to motivate them into action. Remember those days?

As you have probably realized motivating a teenager is not the easiest of tasks... Many of our daughters have mastered the art of manipulation. Finding a way to get what they want, in the way they want it and on their terms. We have to be in tune with what our daughters' hot buttons are. Asking ourselves, "What is she passionate about, what motivates and interests her?"

We can use this information to guide her to wanting to attain a specific goal. As an example, if I want my daughter to spend more time on homework and less time talking with friends online, I need to figure out what will be the benefit to her if she accomplishes it. I know spending more time on studies will benefit her in her future. It will help develop good habits that will contribute to attaining her goals. Just coming out and telling our daughters they cannot speak with friends unless they have finished their school work won't be the most advantageous way to go about it.

We need to help our daughters convince themselves that it's to their benefit. If our daughter buys into the fact that she can accomplish great things by making better choices, applying herself to her studies now and sacrificing some social time with friends will be a better path vs. punishing her if she spends too much time socializing. Many of our daughters as they grow into teenagers think they know what's best for themselves. Of course they want to do it their way.

Offering to help study with them and be

involved with what tests and projects they have coming up can motivate them to be a better planner and become more organized. If they go over the specifics with you it helps them plan and get a better handle on their responsibilities.

They have to think it's their idea to spend more time doing schoolwork than texting. We have to convince our daughters they have to take ownership for their actions. When they choose to make sacrifices that will benefit their future, they will be more inclined to move forward in a postitive way.

There are books that can inspire our daughters. Do some research and find some biographies on strong, successful women, some who have overcome incredible obstacles. They will offer empowerment and motivation. Give our daughters a few options, and encourage them to read and discuss the books with you. It will benefit them greatly. I have a list of some books that helped influence myself and my daughters to positive thinking and encouragement on page 150.

I never gave my children monetary rewards when they did well in school. I felt it was their responsibility to do the best they could. I wanted to develop them into kids who wanted to do well and apply themselves without dangling a carrot in front of them. My younger two daughters at times were disappointed I did not offer rewards. I let them know that they should feel accomplished if they do well in school and the habits they formed would help motivate them to be more successful in their future.

It was difficult when some of their friends would get money or cell phones or game systems when they did what was expected of them to begin with, or worse, a new car just for turning sixteen.

I wanted my children to be motivated to do well in school regardless of the prize. The actual prize was already received when they did a good job.

It's imperative our daughters take ownership in their lives.

- Showing that we believe in them will do a lot to build their self-confidence.

- Making suggestions on activities that they can do to put themselves closer to their goals will be empowering.

- Setting up experiences that will help keep her motivated.

I have always encouraged my teens to get a job after school. The experience they had was something we could never put a price tag on. My teens got experience being on time, receiving a paycheck, having to answer to another adult, and getting a little understanding that life in the work place isn't always fair. Using their job as a means to develop stronger communication skills was invaluable.

Having part time jobs facilitated in their independence and growing up. I also suggested that they put half of what they earned in a savings account allowing them to spend the other half. It was a discipline my parents instilled in me and all of my siblings when we were growing up. It paid off. We were all hard working teens who had a good idea of the value of money.

Yes, we may have been motivated by money but, more importantly, the jobs helped us become independent, responsible and motivated. We never realized we were gaining so many worthwhile experiences working for minimum wage...

> Cheer her on and convince her
> there isn't anything she cannot accomplish
> if she sets her mind to it,
> if she is willing to take the steps
> to accomplish her goals.

It's our responsibility to help develop an independent, strong, confident, positive daughter. If our daughters have all of the above characteristics but no motivation to do anything, it's like an airplane without fuel. We need to figure out what will work in order to motivate them to soar. With motivation, we will help to prepare them to ready themselves for life. By spending quality time with our daughters we will get to know what she really enjoys. What her true aspirations are. Encourage them to think about their future with an open, positive, focused mind.

Be careful not to shoot down any ideas our daughters come up with as career choices. It could possibly backfire. There are so many possible career choices that our daughters haven't been exposed to yet.

As they mature they will have more experiences and information to better define their career choices and goals. Our job is to motivate them and help them develop the skills they need to be successful in whatever they choose.

> Girls can control their futures with positive influences, experiences and determination.

"Always put your best foot forward,
because you never know
where your next step may lead you."

Stephan Labossiere
Certified Coach and Motivational Speaker

Hygiene and Health

Chapter Ten

HYGIENE: What we do to keep ourself and our surroundings clean in order to maintain good health.

HEALTH: Choices we make with eating, excercise, sleep to keep our bodies strong and working properly.

Just when we thought we understood our daughters... Then comes puberty, with pimples, mood swings, attitude, awkwardness, not to mention hormones.

We have already lived through many of the challenges our daughters will encounter. Now, it's our chance to lend understanding, reassurance and above all patience.

There will be days when our daughters may not want to shower or even get out of bed. It's our responsibility to assist them in developing good habits. Keeping a clean body will not only make them feel better it will help with acne and body odor as well.

Sometimes it just happens overnight. All of a sudden our daughters start to take more interest in what they look like, becoming interested in wearing makeup or spending hours to fix their dreaded "Bed Head"... Until that time comes, encourage good hygiene, healthy eating, sleep and exercise habits. Helping them to make healthy food choices is a lifelong, valuable lesson. It can be challenging to get them to understand that living on pizza, ice-cream and chocolate chip cookies alone will not suffice. Fruits, Veggies, water, proteins, yogurt, calcium rich foods are important, too! It's OK to splurge a little, but having balance is key.

Eating the right foods can help with a number of issues that they will encounter. You may notice at times our daughters will use food as an escape or a stress relief. It's much healthier and more productive to engage them in other ways to assist with the pressures they're dealing with by developing good eating, sleeping and excercise habits.

Suggest working together to plan and create some healthy delicious meals. It's a great way to have our daughters take interest in what goes into their bodies and another way to spend quality time with them.

This is a good time to get started with an exercise routine that you can both participate in. You can take yoga classes together, go for bike rides, jog, dance, or do a work out video. It doesn't have to cost a lot of money but this helps you both feel connected. Also the exercise helps relieve some of your stress. I always found my daughters opened up about what's on their mind during long bike rides where they were able to escape a little, relax and feel a little more free.

> Help to make our daughters
> feel beautiful on the inside
> so they can radiate that beauty
> on the outside.
> Their confidence and happiness
> will shine through.

Our teens have probably already started shaving, legs and armpits. Some may want to bleach facial hair or pluck eyebrows. It's natural for them to take pride in their appearance. Remember it's our responsibility to help them through this difficult time in their lives and help them to feel beautiful inside and out. Most will be very self-conscious. It's OK to ask them if they want your help. I find, sometimes they welcome my advice and other times they rolled their eyes. Their mood swings have a lot to do with the influx of hormones, insecurities and big changes their bodies are going through.

Piercings have become a pretty big thing. As a parent it's up to you to discuss the rules you have set in place. Tattoos were another thing I am not crazy about. I saw an interview once with Reggie Bush (Professional Football Player) when he was asked why he didn't have any tattoos he replied, **"There isn't anything I want badly enough to look at every day tattooed on my body."** I was impressed with Reggie, knowing the peer pressure put on many athletes today to fit in and be cool. He was secure in himself and wasn't afraid to voice his oppinions.

I encourage my daughters to really think it through and try not to let the excitement or pressure to fit in get the best of them. They may think they want a tattoo or piercings to fit in with other kids or to feel grown up. Sometimes, it's only a matter of time before they change their mind and the idea becomes a passing phase. As a parent I personally will never approve of a tattoo. Tattoos are just one of the things I don't like. But, everyone has their own opinion. Each of us has to determine for ourselves what we will allow our teens to do.

I suggest making them wait until they are eighteen or graduated from High School or even college before they make a permanent change to their bodies. They mature so much during these teen years they may regret having done it.

Part of good health is getting enough sleep. Consider when our daughters are moody, cranky and just plain mean. Don't take it personally. Sleep deprivation alone can make anyone cranky. Getting enough sleep is challenging for teens. Their schedules are full and their bodies need a lot of sleep that they seldom get. When they have a chance (on a weekend) allow them to make up for some of the sleep they may have lost during the week. It will help not only with their attitudes but keeping them healthy too.

> Choosing my battles
> is a brilliant concept
> that has served me well.

When emotions are running high it may be difficult to deal with. Try taking a step back and consider all of the daily stresses our daughters face. Find ways to help them understand that most of the issues will work themselves out. Encourage them to find a way to ride out some of the emotions. Suggest a long run, a hot relaxing bath and a good night's sleep to help them find a different perspective in the morning.

As our daughters become young women, they will notice all of their peers may be at different stages in development. There is usually the girl who develops breasts and gets her period long before the norm. As well as, some girls who still look much younger than their actual age. Discuss this in a supportive way regardless of where your daughter fits in. It's not easy being on either end of the spectrum. It's vital for them to learn to be sensitive to other girls. If your daughter is the early developed one, she may get a lot of attention from the boys. Don't let her think this is the kind of attention that defines who she is.

Be Comforting and encourage them into believing they are so much more than what their body looks like.

"The power of intuitive understanding
will protect you from harm
until the end of your day."

- Lao Tzu -
Ancient Philosopher and Writer

How To Protect Herself

Chapter Eleven

PROTECTION: Taking precautions to keep ourselves safe. How we stand up to protect our bodies, minds and our hearts.

Did you ever have the hair on the back of your neck stand straight up or get an uneasy feeling about someone you just met? This feeling is called intuition. Each of us is born with it. Some develop their intuition stronger than others. When practiced it can protect us. It's imperative that we explain to our daughters that if something or someone doesn't feel right, it probably isn't.

Help them develop their own radar. Communicate with our daughters on how to avoid places where they would be in danger. Help them to understand they should always be aware of their surroundings and how to avoid looking vulnerable or lost. These are some suggestions that may keep our daughters safe. We cannot always be there with them.

Our daughters must not be naïve, they may be in a situation where their lives depend on their actions. It's imperative to discuss if there is someone who may be acting inappropriately, or giving us or our daughters the creeps... There are many vile people in this world, and some of these creeps look handsome and fit in well with everyone else. It would be great if we could tell a bad person by what they look like. Not so, there are men like Ted Bundy who used their charm and looks to get young women to let their guard down. It's a reality that some men and women on the internet are posing as teenagers who are really adults hoping to lure our trusting daughters away.

How can we help our daughters to have a great life and keep themselves safe? Making them aware of dangers as well as teaching them some signs to watch out for is vital. It's our responsibility to teach them how to protect themselves. I remind my daughters often that if someone is trying to get them into a car against their will, they are to do whatever they can to avoid being taken. Respect for the perpetrator goes out the window. If approached, kick, scream, scratch their eyes out, bite them, do whatever it takes to avoid getting into the car. More than likely the perpetrator will give up and move on to a less adversarial target.

I don't like scaring my daughters, but I need them to understand, if the perpetrator gets them into the car, they will probably get severely brutalized and in many cases, killed. Anything they can do to avoid being taken may save their lives. There is a class my daughters and I took a number of years ago called "Rape Aggression Defense" (RAD). I believe it's a national program usually run by Police Officers. It teaches self-defense in ways that every female should know. Search for classes in your local area. They also offer classes for children. It was an experience that we participated in together and gave us additional confidence in the power we had to protect ourselves. The class gave me some peace of mind. I felt my daughters were made more aware of bad situations they could come across and how to get out of them safely.

Forewarn our daughters, sometimes people we know and trust may want to cause harm. Learning to trust their instincts will help. It may be a boy they date or a friend who may want to be more than just a friend. Someone may be under the influence of alcohol or drugs and may try to force themselves on our daughters. I found discussing these situations to be extremely helpful.

All the while trying to prevent our daughters from becoming paranoid and neurotic, that's an enormous challenge with life these days.

Protecting our daughters hearts may be out of our control. We cannot manipulate the actions others will take towards them. We can however, help build our daughters' confidence and self-worth to allow them to be stronger and more able to protect not only their bodies but their minds and hearts too.

Early on in my parenting, I thought it was normal and acceptable for my daughters to have a boyfriend. I soon realized it's significantly more valuable for my daughters to develop friend relationships with boys instead. There is no specific age I can recommend to give your daughters permission to date, it will be your decision as her parent. Teenage girls experience such crucial growth in their teen years and having an intimate relationship with a boy can truly hinder that growth.

I've seen many girls get involved way too deep, making their life evolve around their boyfriend. They miss out on many fun experiences as a teenager. It's much healthier to have friends that are boys and not necessarily be in a steady monogamous relationship. Let's be realistic, it can be difficult to convince our daughters to buy into this way of thinking. I believe it's worth the effort.

Our daughters virtue is something boys really do need to respect. Let's face facts, there is a fine line between "Love and Lust." We have to help our daughters not to depend on a boys attention to make her feel loved and important. Our daughters have so much to offer the world. Being in a serious relationship before they are emotionally ready can be extremely detrimental to their psyche.

To put it bluntly, having sex at a young age can leave many hidden scars. Some parents think it's OK to let their daughter be in a serious relationship as a teenager. I know a number of Mom's who have allowed their daughters to go on birth control pills as young as 13 because they were sexually active. While other Moms turn a blind eye and expect that their daughters will know better. Please, let's not be naïve. Kids are having sex as early at eleven. Their bodies are maturing earlier yet their minds are still young.

Inevitably, our daughters will eventually date. Forbidding them to see a certain boy usually doesn't go over very well, in fact, I have seen it backfire and go the opposite direction a number of times. Suggest they hold off on having sex until she is certain they are emotionally ready for it, not just physically ready, and not because everyone else is having sex. It really is OK to be a virgin throughout high school and longer. It's vital to talk to our daughters about how special they are and how important it is to respect their bodies. Giving their bodies to a boy they think they are in love with will not be the best decision for them as a teen.

Having sex today puts our daughters at risk for many health issues, not just unwanted pregnancy but AIDS and other potentially life threatening sexually transmitted diseases (STD's) that can affect them negatively for the rest of their lives. I suggest if your daughter is having sex, encourage her to use precautions; at a minimum, condoms and birth control pills. Do whatever you can to keep open communications with her. Helping her to understand that although you may not agree with her choice, you are always there for her and that you love her very much and want her to be safe.

"A mother's love for her child
is like nothing else in the world.
It knows no law, no pity,
it dares all things, and crushes down
remorselessly
all that stand in its path."

Agatha Christie
Author

"Most fears of rejection rest on the desire for approval from other people. Don't base your self-esteem on their opinions."

Harvey MacKay
Motivational Speaker and Author

EMOTIONS
CHAPTER TWELVE

EMOTIONS: The feelings we have of joy, sorrow, fear, hate, the way we express them.

Nobody said raising a teen daughter was going to be easy. I write this chapter today as tears stream down my face. I left my daughter's school after a Mother's Day Breakfast, "A day where I was to be celebrated, or so I thought." My daughters treatment of me was dismissive, almost as if she didn't want me to be there at all. There will be days that our daughters will wish we were non-existent. I don't ever doubt her love for me yet, drying our tears is something we Moms have to endure from time to time.

Our daughters emotions run high between wanting to fit in, pressures to be liked, pressures with school work, lack of sleep... LACK OF SLEEP... did I mention LACK OF SLEEP...

Raising a teenage daughter has many trying times. Don't despair, one day they will look back with fond memories and realize how truly lucky they are to have a Mom like us... Remember this thought when we are experiencing the hurt and disappointment of not being appreciated, or respected. Afterall, we are raising, or should I say, "Playing" with teenage dynamite.

Being a teenager with emotions all over the map, it's hard for them to reign it in at times. I try not to take their behavior too personally, although, I don't want to give them an excuse either. Keeping this all in proper perspective helps cushion the blows.

It's helpful to have a significant other or a family member who can step in when an emotional situation happens between Mother and Daughter. Many times hurtful words are exchanged and emotions can quickly continue to escalate. Our daughters have a good idea of what buttons to press to get the reactions they want from us. Having someone not involved with the situation can be extremely helpful. They can help to defuse the situation before it gets out of hand. Prior to any confrontational incident occurring it's important to discuss with your significant other or family member, how you want them to step in and offer them suggestions as to what you may want them to do.

Allow for everyone's emotions to cool down before continuing the discussion. Take a step back to realize what went wrong and how things can go better next time. In some cases our daughters will apologize and take responsibility without being prompted, other times we may be the one who has to apologize for losing our cool. In times like these I call for a "Do Over!"

> Calling a "DO OVER" may help get everyone back on track. Taking a step back when either of you said something that you didn't mean, and ask permission to start over.

Mood swings are as much a part of the teenage years as braces and biology. There are so many things that contribute to mood swings, like the need to fit in, or the influx of hormones. Many times we may not see the cause as much as the result of all of the pressures building. There may be times when our daughters behaviors won't fit there usual actions.

Our daughters' behavior could become volatile, with higher than usual highs, or exhibit bouts of depression. Some teens may start to withdraw or become anxious; they may have trouble sleeping or they may sleep too long. These are some signs to look out for, something more serious may be going on.

This may be time to ask for an outside professional's help. These are very real feelings our daughters may be experiencing. Teenagers, have so much more growth to experience and their coping skills are not always at their strongest or fully developed. It may be challenging to figure out what is really going on with our daughters.

> There is no shame in asking for outside help.

If your gut is telling you there is something not right with your daughters behavior, it's time to address it. There are psychologists who specialize in working with teens who may be able to communicate with our daughters, offering guidance and peace of mind. Our daughters could be trying to handle a situation on their own without realizing that the problem may be larger than they are equipped to deal with. We have to look for the signs that they may be reaching out even though it may feel as if they are pulling away.

> Please, follow your gut instinct

"The future belongs to those who believe in the beauty of their dreams."

Eleanor Roosevelt
American politician, diplomat, and activist.
First Lady of the United States

"Be who you are and say what you feel because those who mind, don't matter and those who matter, don't mind."

Dr. Seuss
American writer and illustrator

Sexual Orientation
Chapter Thirteen

SEXUAL ORIENTATION: (Being Gay) Romantic sexual attraction between a person of the same sex. (Transgender) refers to idenity and gender expression.

    I thought I had completed all of my chapters when I realized I didn't write about Teens who are gay or transgender. None of my children are gay or transgender, so I wasn't initially focused on this chapter. I started thinking about some of the girls and boys I grew up with who are gay. I also have relatives whom I love and respect very much and I couldn't imagine not accepting and loving them for who they are.

When I was growing up, I faced a very different world than our teens do today, although I believe sadly at times our teens today face a much harder life.

I knew teens who were gay when I was a teenager, some of them didn't even know what it meant. Can you imagine a young teen girl who was never exposed or learned about being gay trying to struggle through her teenage years with the feelings she has?

Having much of society tell them they are perverse. I understand some people today are fearful and think being gay is wrong. I disagree strongly.

You may never as a parent have to experience this with your own teens, but many parents do. I believe it's our responsibility to help our teens be more accepting of people who may be different than they are.

Having discussions about gay and transgender teens may be a way to help our daughters figure out how they feel about it. There is information on the internet to help you get informed. The world is changing but I don't think quickly enough.

I read too many articles about teens who have committed suicide after they were ostracized and bullied because they were gay or transgender. That is absolutely unacceptable.

With social media being so embedded within our teens' daily lives, it must be very hard for anyone to figure out who they truly are with so many examples of who others think they should be. Society seems to want to put everyone in a nice neat box instead of embracing and accepting our uniqueness.

When I was a teenager, a friend of mine was gay. I wasn't truly sure what it meant to be gay at the time but I figured out she liked girls instead of boys. In the area she lived in there wasn't much exposure to gay people. She shared with me that as young as 10 years old, she knew she did not like boys and that she was attracted to girls. She initially thought there was something very wrong with her.

It was comforting to know that she had a close relationship with her Mom and was able to discuss this openly and explain her feelings. Her Mom offered understanding and complete acceptance. There are many teens who aren't so fortunate and don't have anyone they can turn to.

> Now imagine if this girl was your daughter. Do you think she would be able to talk to you about being gay?

Can you imagine spending much of your life pretending to be someone you are not? Whether it's because of the way people will treat you or because you feel you are somehow perverse and others won't accept or understand you?

I have known girls that have never been able to come out and be who they truly are for fear of rejection or worse. It saddens me to think there are many girls who are in this situation.

⁂

Years ago I worked with a young guy who was gay, and we got into a discussion with a few other co-workers about how we felt about gay people.

He shared with us that when he was about twelve years old he told his Mom that he was gay. She told him that she had known he was gay since he was a little boy and that she was happy he was able to tell her. She said she didn't know how to bring the subject up to him and was glad he felt comfortable enough to discuss it with her. He was fortunate to have a Mom like he did.

He asked me how I would feel if my son or daughter told me that they were gay. I think I surprised him with my answer. I told him I would honestly be sad but not for the reason he thought.

I told him I would be sad because I knew how difficult it would be with so many ignorant people in this world and how badly they may treat my child. I told him my love for my children would not change. I would accept them regardless of their sexual preference. I still feel the same way and always will.

My hopes for them would be that they find happiness, respect and love with themselves and the people they have in their lives.

I do not believe we have a choice. I believe we are born with our sexual orientation predetermined and the God that I love and believe in is accepting and loving of everyone who is a good person.

When one of my daughters was three years old we had gone to a birthday party for an adult friend of ours who was gay. I hadn't thought about discussing this with her before we went to the party.

My daughter had already had a friendship with this man and felt very comfortable with him each time we were all together.

The party was a lot of fun and our friend had a princess birthday cake and a crown. His partner was the one who gave him the party and throughout the day they were affectionate towards each other holding hands and embracing.

On our drive home from the party as my daughter sat in her car seat, I could tell she was thinking very hard about something. I asked if she had fun at the party and she replied, "Yes it was really fun!" Then very seriously she asked if she could tell me something. I said, "Of course." Out of the mouths of babes my daughter said "I think Jordan (we will call him) sometimes likes to be a boy and sometimes likes to be a girl." I asked how she felt about that, she replied "That's OK, isn't it?"

I told her yes, sometimes boys will be in love with girls (like Mommy and Daddy) and sometimes boys will be in love with boys, also girls can fall in love with girls, too.

I hadn't really thought through my answer but it seemed to be good enough for her at the time.

I have always chosen to discuss the differences in people and how we should accept them as long as they are good people. It doesn't matter what nationality they are, what religion they are, what color their skin is, or what their sexual orientation.

> Please be open minded, there is too much fear and hate in this world.

Taking the lead and accepting people for who they are is an action none of us will regret.

I hope as parents we choose to be accepting of our teenagers sexual preference and be supportive of their individuality. It may be challenging at times, but anything that is worthwhile doesn't usually come easy.

Our teenagers are only teens for a short time. Although it may seem like an eternity, the time passes so quickly. Let's make it an amazing experience for everyone.

Give ourselves a break, not one of us is perfect. There may always be something we could have handled better.   All we can ask of ourselves is to do the best we can. Above all let our daughters know how proud of them we are and how much we love them. It's essential to have fun and make memories with our daughters. The time we have with them is precious. Life moves so quickly. Before we know it they will be off on their first day of high school, then college, marriage and more… It may seem like an enormous task to be blessed with a daughter that we have been responsible for molding into an incredible young lady and truly prepare her to be independent of us.

I find it bittersweet to see our daughters pass through their teenage years into adulthood, but I wouldn't change it for the world.

Preparing them as best we can
is all anyone can ask for.
I don't know any girls today who wished
their moms had loved them less.
Do you?

Let's show our teen daughters how much we love them by taking the time to understand them. Spend quality time now and make memories that will last all of us a lifetime. Being the Mom they can count on is an incredibly valuable goal. Help them to believe that they can control their futures with positive influences and experiences.

The world will come to know our daughters as Brave, Smart and Beautiful inside and out.

Thoughts

We ARE at times going to lose our temper.

We ARE going to say things we regret.

We ARE going to sometimes not have a clue how to communicate with them.

> When we realize things haven't gone as well as we had hoped, remember to call for a "Do Over!"

It's OK to apologize and let our daughters know we didn't handle a specific situation as well as we had hoped. Ask to discuss the issue with a clear head. Think through what it is that we really want to convey. Most of all we as Moms have to find a way to let our daughters know we love them and really want what we believe is best for them. Our daughters may think we don't have a clue, but we were teenagers once and even though situations may be different the feelings we experienced were very similar.

I made a promise to myself at seventeen that I would be the best Mom I could possibly be. I am grateful and proud to have kept my promise.

I had many challenges as a young mother, but was always determined to do the best I could for all of my children.

I gave birth to my first daughter (Jessica) two weeks after I turned eighteen, my son Douglas was born when I was twenty-one, my next daughter (Caitlyn) born when I was twenty-seven.

I became a step Mom to a teenage daughter (Christine) and my stepson Brian, when I was thirty-three. Then gave birth to our youngest daughter (Kylie) when I was thirty-five.

I have been blessed to have two incredible student exchange daughters through The Rotary Club of Weston: (Christin) from Borken, Germany when I was forty-six and (Chiara) from Brescia, Italy two years later.

I have been privileged to experience many teenagers turn into amazing, confident young adults. I understand all too well how quickly this time goes. From nursery school, elementary, to middle school, high school, college and marriage, there isn't a day that goes by I don't look back on those little innocent faces and think about how proud I am to be their mother. How impressed I am at the independent, loving, responsible, people they have become.

Please don't waste the precious time you have with your children, cherish every moment. It's never too late to share quality, fun times with them.

On the next page I have a list of some ideas that may help get things started. There are so many things you can do together that doesn't have to cost a lot of money. Only your time. Go ahead, the memories will be worth every effort...

> What does a memory mean....
> Make an impact with intention and enthusiasm.

Making Memories Now

- Bake a cake, just because
- Plan & Prepare a meal; encourage them to come up with an idea
- Take a cooking lesson
- Simple pedicures & manicures
- Dance in the rain
- Volunteer at a soup kitchen
- Create new hairstyles
- Speak in a different accent, see how long you can take the conversation
- Exercise: walk, jog, play hopscotch, shoot baskets, jump rope, play catch
- Walk on the beach and collect shells or watch the sunset
- Read a book together, out loud; take turns by chapter or page
- Pick up a hobby like photography
- Schedule an afternoon with just the two of you. If you have more than one daughter plan the activity separately.
- Plan a MOTHER-DAUGHTER Skip Day No phones, No work, No school, Just fun!

"Love them Unconditionally
Acceptance and Patience
are Key..."

Diane Grant

From the Kids

Notes from my children I wanted to share

"Mom, I just wanted you to know that no woman will ever be more respected or loved by me than you. You are always and have always been the most important person to me and that is probably why I have always been more affected by how you thought of me, whether good or bad. I was always afraid to let you down.

I feel so good right now because I have let out my stupid feelings and opened up to you. It is like a weight has been lifted. I am sorry that I have let this affect the way I have treated you in the past. It was almost like I thought you disliked me. So I distanced myself from you to keep myself from getting hurt.

You never did anything to make me feel this way, it was all just me. I know I was wrong now and believe me things will be different. I am so sorry for thinking this way.

I Love You...

Remember I am not great with my words but I am trying to be. You mean a lot to me and I am the person that I am right now because you did the right thing as a parent to get me here.

I am not done growing and learning. I think you did a great job and you have grown to be a wonderful, smart, beautiful woman.

from the kids cont'd

I love you so much and you are the world to me.
I am getting a little bit emotional now so I have to stop
typing before I cry. I hope you understand what I am
trying to let you know. I wish I had not held
back from you for so long.
I love you."
"Every day you should wake up and know you have
accomplished great things by just bringing us through
this world as well as you have." "Now you can finally
have it returned with everything you have now.
You deserve everything…"

Love, *Jessica*

"I can't begin to tell you how much you mean to me!
It seems that no matter what you have going on you
are always there for me. Thank you!
I guess everything happens for a reason, because I
don't know what I would do without you in my life.
I admire you greatly; you are a fabulous Mother,
Step-Mother, and Grandma!
I hope you have a fabulous day.
we are thinking of you & Love you!"

XOXOXO *Christine*

Thank you for always being here for me
whenever I need you, and
always showing me how much you love me.
I'm proud to say you're my Momma and
I really do like how I look more and more like
you every day, I Love You

Love Always *Caitlyn Michelle*

"Mothers and their children are in a category
all their own.
There's no bond so strong in the entire world.
No love so instantaneous and forgiving."
- Gail Tsukiyama...
I would like to thank my mother so much for
being there through thick and thin,
no matter what!
For giving me unconditional love, support,
and care for thirteen years and nine months
before and for the many years to come.
She is a wonderful and a beautiful woman
who amazes me on how she always
makes everything better with
brownie sundaes, warm hugs,
and great words of advice…
even though it's not always taken.
And I know I speak for all of her children
when I say we have the best mom ever!
Happy Mother's Day Momma
and to all the wonderful moms out there!

Love *Kylie*

from the kids cont'd

Words can't begin to describe how grateful
I am for all you have done for me
throughout these past 29 years,
I Love You. *Douglas*

You go so over and beyond!
We could not be more thankful for you.
Thank you for loving us and making us your own!
We love you so much and
hope you have the most spectacular Mother's Day!
XOXO *Brian and Daughter-in-law Taylor*

I have no words to describe how grateful
and lucky I am to be a part of your wonderful family.
I really hope you enjoyed my stay as much as
I enjoyed mine, because you deserve only the best
and no matter how far away I am,
I will always keep you in my heart forever!
Thank you for being such good parents
to me as if I were your own child.
For giving me the feeling to be loved
from the beginning on.
I Love You.
Your German Daughter *Christin*

I can't believe that I'm leaving. I can't believe that 10 months past, but what I really can't believe is how lucky I was that you picked me.
When I got here I was so excited to start this new life, trying to imagine how it was going to be.
Well, I was wrong about everything that I thought.
I could never imagine that I was going to be and feel part of this amazing family. And yes, you're all amazing, because even if at times you can't stand each other you always love each other. And that's what family is
supposed to mean: caring about each other no matter what happened the day before. Everyone has their own defects, especially me, but you made me feel comfortable with them, without judging me but just helping me. You have no idea how much I grew as a person and that was possible thanks to you, not to the rotary club, not to the school, but to you. Living in a family that is not yours gives you the opportunity to see things from a different perspective, but living with this family gave me so much more.
I saw how much a parent does for her/his children and how much sisters care for each other,
even if sometimes they're too proud to admit it.
You all know that I don't want to leave but a part of me can't wait to show the Italian people what I learned here and trust me, I learned a lot. My mom would say that
surely I still have my sarcasm but I can't wait to show her too what I became. This year I was able to put myself in situations that in the past would have scared me,
like speaking in front of an audience,
meeting new people from all over the world,
visiting places that I just dreamed of, to open my mind.
I can't thank you enough for opening your home to me, that is truly the most beautiful thing that someone did for me, and I'm so happy and honored to be able to call this home and you family . Thank you so much for everything, I love you all.

Your Italian Daughter *Chiara*

Recommended Reading

All the Light We Cannot See
By: Anthony Doerr

Awaken the Giant Within
By: Tony Robbins

Lean In
By: Sheryl Sandberg

My Sisters Keeper
By: Jodi Picoult

Pay it Forward
By: Catherine Ryan Hyde

Rich Dad Poor Dad
By: Robert T. Kiyosaki

The 7 Habits of Highly Effective Teens
By: Stephen R. Covey

The Outliers
By: Malcom Gladwell

The Power of Positive Thinking
By: Dr. Norman Vincent Peale

Think and Grow Rich
By: Napoleon Hill

Tuesdays With Morrie
By: Mitch Albom

The Power of Self-Discipline
By: Brian Tracey

Diane Grant

Born in New Rochelle, New York.
Graduated from New Rochelle High School 1983.

Happily married to her best friend,
and love of her life Jim Grant.

Blessed to have six children and seven grandchildren.

Diane is an author, public speaker
and artist living in sunny
South Florida.
She loves spending time
making memories with her family.

www.BraveSmartandBeautiful.com